The Story of

Florence Nightingale

Anita Ganeri

Raintree

www.raintreepublishers.co.uk
Visit our website to find out more information about **Raintree** books.

To order:
☎ Phone 44 (0) 1865 888112
🗎 Send a fax to 44 (0) 1865 314091
💻 Visit the Raintree Bookshop at **www.raintreepublishers.co.uk** to browse our catalogue and order online.

First published in Great Britain by Raintree, Halley Court, Jordan Hill, Oxford OX2 8EJ, part of Pearson Education. Raintree is a registered trademark of Pearson Education Ltd.

© Pearson Education Ltd 2008
The moral right of the proprietor has been asserted.

Editorial: Sian Smith
Design: Kimberley R. Miracle, Big Top and Joanna Hinton-Malivoire
Picture research: Ruth Blair
Production: Duncan Gilbert
Illustrated by Beehive Illustration
Originated by Dot Gradations

Printed and bound in China by Leo Paper Group

ISBN 978 1 4062 1008 8 (hardback)
ISBN 978 14062 1018 7 (paperback)

12 11 10
10 9 8 7 6 5 4 3 2

British Library Cataloguing in Publication Data
Ganeri, Anita, 1961-
  The story of Florence Nightingale
  1. Nightingale, Florence, 1820-1910 - Juvenile literature
  2. Nurses - Great Britain - Biography - Juvenile literature
  3. Crimean War, 1853-1856 - Medical care - Juvenile literature
  I. Title
  610.7'3'092

Acknowledgments
The publishers would like to thank the following for permission to reproduce photographs: ©Alamy pp.5, 4 (Mary Evans Picture Library), 19(Pictorial Press Ltd), 11 (Visual Arts Library, London); ©Antiquarian Images p.10; ©Art Archive p.16; ©Bridgeman p.6; ©Corbis p.13, 15, 17 (Bettmann); ©Getty Images pp.7, 12, 14, 18 (Hulton Archive), 8 (Time Life Pictures) ; ©Photodisc p.4 (Glen Allison)

Cover photograph of Florence Nightingale reproduced with permission of ©Corbis (Bettmann).

Every effort has been made to contact copyright holders of any material reproduced in this book. Any omissions will be rectified in subsequent printings if notice is given to the publisher.

Contents

Some words are printed in bold, **like this**. You can find out what they mean in the glossary.

Who was Florence Nightingale?

This is a photograph of Florence Nightingale. She is dressed in the clothes of Victorian times.

The city of Florence.

Florence Nightingale was born in 1820 in the city of Florence in Italy. Her mother liked the city so much that she named her daughter Florence after it. Later, Florence moved to Britain with her family.

This drawing shows Florence with two women that she trained to be nurses.

For most of Florence's life, Queen Victoria was queen of Britain. In **Victorian** times, hospitals were very dirty and **crowded**. Many **patients** died of **diseases** they caught in hospital. When Florence grew up, she became a famous **nurse**. She worked hard to make hospitals cleaner and healthier. She also taught nurses how to look after patients properly.

Florence's family

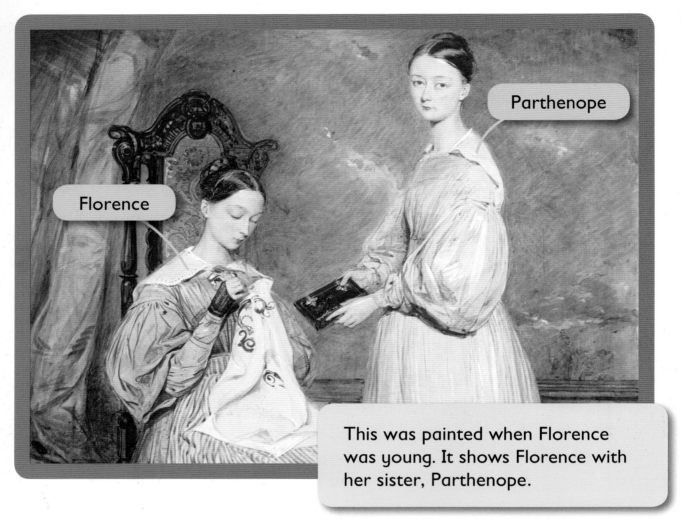

Florence

Parthenope

This was painted when Florence was young. It shows Florence with her sister, Parthenope.

Florence's father was called William Nightingale. Her mother was called Frances. Florence had one sister. Her name was Parthenope, but everyone called her Parthe. Florence's nickname was Flo. The Nightingale family was very rich. They lived in a big house and they had lots of **servants** to look after them.

Embley Park was the big house where the Nightingale family lived.

Flo and Parthe did not go to school. They had lessons at home with their father. Sometimes, Frances took Flo and Parthe to visit poor people in the nearby village. Flo felt sad and wanted to help them. She took them clothes and gave them money to buy food.

Becoming a nurse

From a young age, Florence dreamed of becoming a **nurse**. She wanted to help people who were poor and sick. Her mother did not like the idea of Florence going to work. She wanted her to marry a rich man instead.

But Florence had made up her mind. She
read lots of books about nursing and went to
visit hospitals. Then she got a job running a
hospital in London. Florence worked very hard.
She cleaned every **ward** in the hospital.
She also made sure that her **patients** had
hot food to eat.

The Crimean War

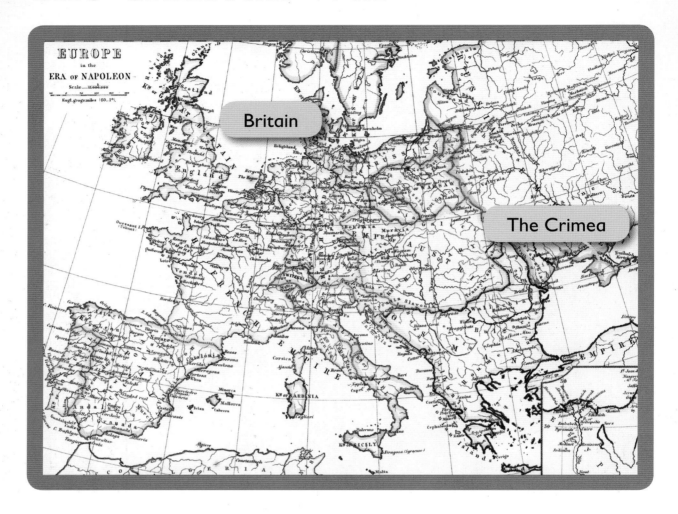

In 1854, Britain went to war with Russia. The war was fought a long way away from Britain in a place called the **Crimea**. It was called the Crimean War. Florence read about the war in the newspaper. She thought that it sounded terrible.

This painting shows fighting during the Crimean War.

Thousands of British soldiers were **wounded** in the fighting. Some were taken to hospital. But the hospitals were dirty and full of **germs** which caused terrible **diseases**. Instead of getting better, many of the wounded soldiers caught these diseases and died.

Florence goes to help

Florence had a friend called Sidney Herbert. He was a **politician**. He asked Florence to go and nurse the **wounded** soldiers. Florence said "yes" at once. She chose some other nurses to go along with her and help.

This is a photograph of Sidney Herbert.

Florence on her journey to Scutari.

Florence had to travel to a place called Scutari in Turkey. This is where the wounded British soldiers were being looked after. It was a long and difficult journey from Britain. Florence and her nurses travelled by land across Europe. Then they sailed in a ship, and many of the nurses were **seasick**.

A dirty hospital

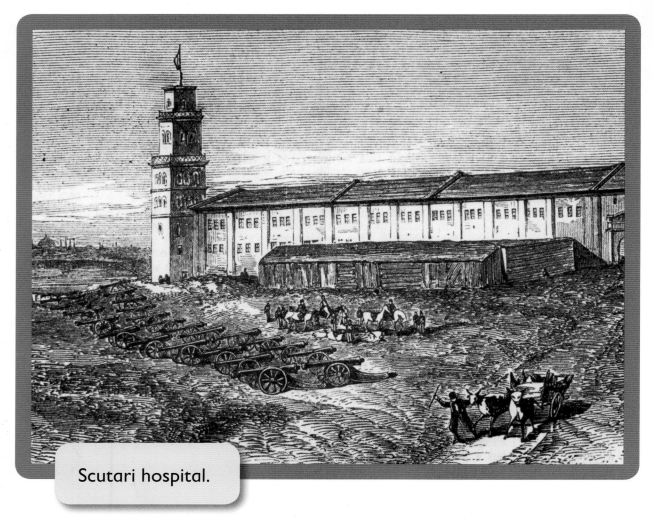

Scutari hospital.

Scutari was a long way away from the **Crimea**. Soldiers who were **wounded** in the fighting had to travel there by boat. When Florence reached the hospital, she was shocked at what she saw. The hospital was dirty and smelly. Some soldiers had to lie on the floor because there were not enough beds. There were no bandages or medicines.

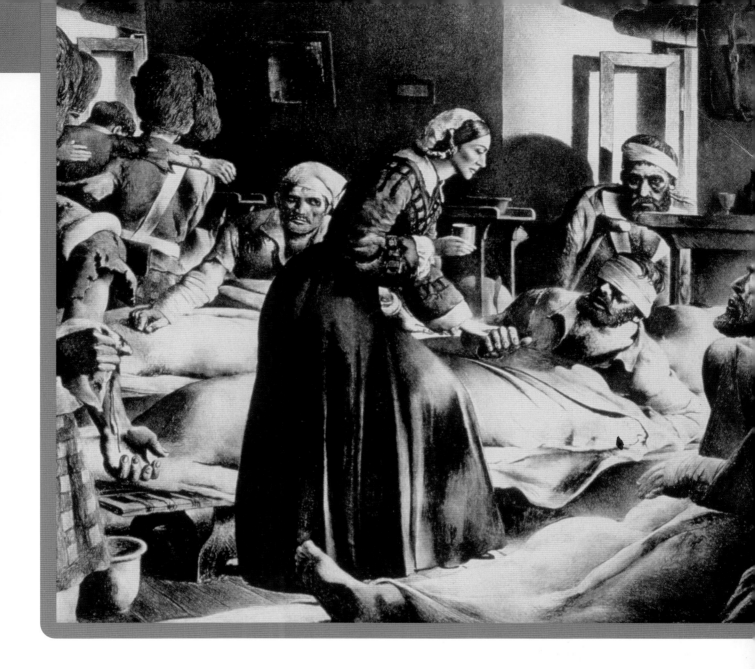

At first, the doctors at the hospital were
not happy to see Florence and her **nurses**.
But they had too many **patients** to look after.
They soon asked Florence for help.

The lady with the lamp

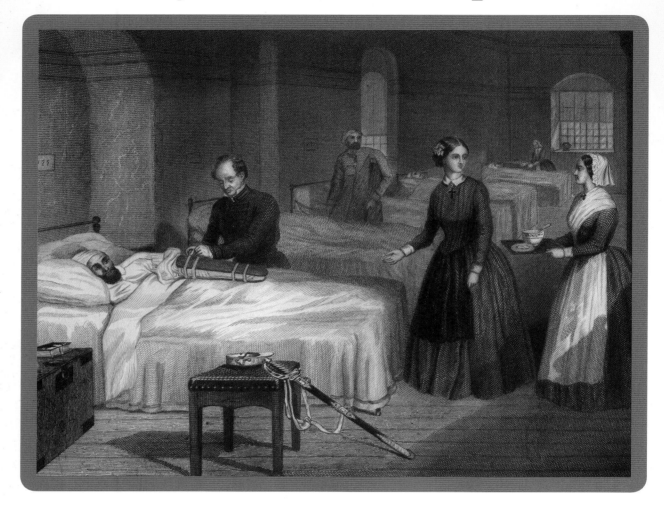

Florence and her **nurses** worked hard. They cleaned the hospital from top to bottom. They put clean sheets on the beds. They bought food, pillows, and candles. Medicines were sent from Britain. There was also a new stove to keep the **patients** warm. All of these things helped the soldiers to get better.

Florence was always kind and gentle to her patients. At night, she walked along the **wards**, holding a lamp in her hand. She talked to and smiled at the soldiers. Sometimes, she held their hands. The soldiers called Florence "the Lady with the Lamp".

Florence goes home

Florence with nurses at her training school in London.

After the war, Florence went home to Britain. She was well-known for her work in the war. Florence went to live in a hotel in London. There, she wrote a book about nursing called *Notes on Nursing*. She also started a school for **nurses**.

Florence died in 1910. She was 90 years old. She was buried near her family. We can learn about her by reading the letters she wrote. We can also look at old photographs and paintings. We remember her for being a caring nurse and for making hospitals more **hygienic** for **patients**.

Teachers' guide

These books have followed the QCA guidelines closely, but space has not allowed us to cover all the information and vocabulary the QCA suggest. Any suggested material not covered in the book is added to the discussion points below. The books can simply be read as information books, or they could be used as a focus for studying the unit. Below are discussion points grouped in pairs of pages, with suggested follow-up activities.

PAGES 4–5

Talk about:
- Famous people and how we know about them. Stress that TV and the Internet are modern innovations and that it is now possible to find out much more about famous people than it used to be – some of them have their own web pages. Explain you are going to study Florence Nightingale who became famous in Victorian times and that at that time the only way to find out about famous people was in newspapers or magazines.

Possible activity:
- Mark the Victorian period in Britain on the class timeline.

PAGES 6–7

Talk about:
- The class system in Victorian times: simply say some people were very rich, some were very poor and there were many levels in between. They all dressed and lived differently and were not expected to move classes. Girls of Florence's family's class were mostly expected to marry and have children. Mostly, only women from lower classes worked, because their families needed the money. Women of Florence's family's class were encouraged to do useful, voluntary work until they married. Discuss adjectives to describe Florence's aims and standing up to her parents: brave, determined, kind, etc.

Possible activity:
- Sorting at least 10 pictures of Victorian and modern clothing into the right sets and discussing why they made their choices.

PAGES 8–9

Talk about:
- Explain that, before Florence Nightingale, nurses were not trained. Most were working class women. Many were good nurses, but Victorian cartoons often showed nurses as incompetent and often dirty and drunk. Point out that Florence did not work in hospitals until she was 33 and that she was not paid for the work she did.

Possible activity:
- Role play: the children are friends and family of the Nightingales. They should discuss whether Florence should be allowed to work in a hospital. Remind them that they are Victorians. Issues to bear in mind: she's is not yet married, it is useful work, but it is nursing (which has a bad reputation) and harder useful work than visiting the poor and will take a lot of time.

PAGES 10–11

Talk about:
- Discuss how far away the Crimea was. Explain people had just found out about the link between germs and disease. Some people understood the link between keeping clean and patients surviving operations, but some doctors and nurses still did not accept the need for clean hospitals.

Possible activity:
- Brainstorm why people did not just accept the ideas about germs and start keeping things clean. (You can only see germs in laboratories under a microscope, so how could they be so dangerous; people would have to change the way they worked, what they wore, and so on. They would

have to employ more people to clean and they would have to spend more money on supplies.)

PAGES 12–13

Talk about:
- How long it took to get to Scutari and how Florence and her nurses travelled. They travelled by coach, train and ship from 21 October to 4 November. The BBC website has a simple map http://www.bbc.co.uk/schools/famouspeople/standard/journeys/nightingale/ You could read the description at http://www.suite101.com/article.cfm/crimean_war/81410/5/

Possible activity:
- Write a short newspaper report on the sea voyage saying what it was like and how you feel about Nightingale and her nurses for going through it.

PAGES 14–15

Talk about:
- Explain how bad the hygiene was. There were thousands of wounded and dying – patients were often just moved on to the bloodstained sheets of the previous patient. Discuss why conditions might be worse in a war hospital: lots more patients, lots of bad wounds, etc. Add to this that the hospital had not been sent enough supplies and there were only the doctors and a few men to remove and bury the dead and keep the hospital clean. Even so, they didn't want the nurses. They thought the 'ladies' would just get in the way and be no help.

Possible activity:
- Brainstorm what the pictures on these pages tell you. What does the picture of the hospital make clear when you know that it was full of casualties? What impression does the picture of Florence Nightingale and the patients give you of Florence and conditions in the hospital when she arrived?

PAGES 16–17

Talk about:
- Explain that there were 38 nurses, as well as Florence, so they made a big difference. Two years after they had arrived, the death rate in the hospital had fallen from 42 per cent to 2 per cent. Also, the newspapers were soon talking about them and their work, which meant they were given supplies and/or the money to buy them. After the activity, discuss how the doctors felt about the nurses after they had been there long enough to make these changes (most of them approved and were grateful).

Possible activity:
- Fill out a before and after chart for the picture on page 15 and the picture on page 16, to list the ways that the nurses improved things for the soldiers.

PAGES 18–19

Talk about:
- Discuss which was more important, Florence Nightingale's work in the Crimea or setting up training schools for nurses in the UK (which was the start of all nurses having to be qualified). Which has had most impact on our lives now? Does that make it the most important?

Possible activity:
- Work in groups to make a cartoon biography of the main points of Florence's life using sequencing words such as 'before', 'after', 'when' and 'then' and using the pictures in the book as reference material to make each picture as accurate as possible.

Possible visit

The Florence Nightingale Museum in London has exhibitions about the life and work of Florence Nightingale, including artefacts, many pictures and some of Florence's letters and books. (http://www.florence-nightingale.co.uk/details.htm will give the latest contact details, opening times and a map.)

Find out more

Books

Florence Nightingale, Lucy Letherbridge
(Usborne Publishing, 2004)

*How Do We Know About? Florence Nightingale
and the Crimean War,* Jane Shuter (Heinemann
Library, 2003)

Start-up History: Florence Nightingale,
Stewart Ross (Evans Brothers, 2006)

The Life of Florence Nightingale,
Emma Lynch (Heinemann Library, 2005)

Websites

www.bbc.co.uk/schools/famouspeople/standard/nightingale/index.shtml
Click through scenes from Florence Nightingale's life or answer the quiz.

www.florence-nightingale.co.uk
A museum website about the famous nurse.

www.florence-nightingale.co.uk /index.php
This website for the Florence Nightingale Museum has activities to do,
as well as information about their exhibitions.

Glossary

Crimea place in Europe on the shore of the Black Sea

crowded when a place has lots of people in it

diseases illnesses that are caused by germs

germs tiny living things that can cause diseases

hygienic clean and healthy

nurse someone who looks after sick people. To nurse means to work as a nurse, looking after sick people.

patients sick people who are in hospital

politician person who works for the government

seasick sickness caused by the rocking movement of a boat

servant person who works in another person's house

Victorian Victorian times were the times in history when Victoria was queen of England. This was over one hundred years ago.

ward part of a hospital that has beds for patients

wounded another word for injured, or hurt

Index